UNDERSTANDING
SCREEN
ADDICTION

UPFRONT HEALTH

Published in the United States of America by Cherry Lake Publishing
Ann Arbor, Michigan
www.cherrylakepublishing.com

Reading Adviser: Marla Conn MS, Ed., Literacy specialist, Read-Ability, Inc.

Photo Credits: ©Mladen Zivkovic/Getty Images, cover, ©iStockphoto/Getty Images, 1, ©Image Source/Getty Images, 5, ©Blend Images/Getty Images, 9, ©Rokas Tenys/Shutterstock, 10, ©drbimages/Getty Images, 13, ©iStockphoto/Getty Images, 15, ©fstop123/Getty Images, 19, ©Hero Images/Getty Images, 20, ©Alena Ozerova/Shutterstock, 22, ©Tong_stocker/Shutterstock, 23, ©Cavan Images RF/Getty Images, 25, ©iStockphoto/Getty Images, 27, ©iStockphoto/Getty Images, 29, ©Tong_stocker/Shutterstock, 30

Library of Congress Cataloging-in-Publication Data has been filed and is available at catalog.loc.gov

Cherry Lake Publishing would like to acknowledge the work of The Partnership for 21st Century Learning.
Please visit *www.p21.org* for more information.

Printed in the United States of America
Corporate Graphics

ABOUT THE AUTHOR

Renae Gilles is an author, editor, and ecologist from the Pacific Northwest. She has a bachelor's degree in humanities from Evergreen State College and a master's in biology from Eastern Washington University. Renae and her husband currently live in the Northeast with their two daughters, dog, and flock of backyard chickens.

TABLE OF CONTENTS

The World of Screen Addiction

In today's world, screens are everywhere. There is a television and a computer in almost every U.S. home. There might be a laptop and a tablet or two, as well. Most adults and teens carry a cell phone. These devices are powerful tools. Computers and phones help us do work and communicate. Technology allows people to express themselves. Phones and televisions keep people entertained with games, music, shows, and movies. Yet these screens can also become harmful. Too much screen time can damage a person's body and mind.

It can be hard to imagine life before screens. Communication took a little bit more time. People kept busy with work and household chores. More time was spent doing

As screen time is increasing, participation in sports is decreasing among kids and teens.

group activities. People joined clubs. Families read books out loud to each other. In the early 1900s, people listened to radio shows. Before long, most homes had a television too. The first personal computer was invented in the 1970s. Computers did not become a household item until the late 1990s. This is when cell phones started to become common, as well. The first cell phones were mobile phones. Mobile phones let people make and receive calls while on the go. Now cell phones are like miniature computers. Smartphones let people surf the internet, use apps, play games, and much more.

The Business of Screens

There is a booming business behind screens. Each year, more than 1 billion cell phones are sold. Almost 200 million tablets and 300 million computers are sold each year, as well. Americans spend more than $30 billion on video games annually. Companies spend millions of dollars for ads to be seen on **social media**. *This includes websites like Facebook, Instagram, and Twitter. The main goal of most companies is to make money. Companies want people to use their apps and buy more devices, including phones and tablets. Some companies hire people to design products, such as apps, that are addicting to use. Designers use colors, shapes, and sounds that are appealing. It is important to be aware of these methods. Awareness can help prevent screen addiction.*

Screen technology has advanced very quickly. People are still figuring out what is healthy. Today, the average American spends 10 hours each day looking at a screen. Americans watch TV and check social media. Many people play video games. People spend more time with screens than they do on personal grooming, housework, cooking, and eating combined.

Screens are a normal part of most people's lives. For some of these people, screen time can become a powerful **addiction**. Screen addiction is not quite like an addiction to drugs or alcohol. Using a screen is not an illegal activity. But too much screen use can have a very negative effect on a person's life.

Learning with Technology

Screens aren't just in people's homes. Technology is now in classrooms too. A classroom might have tablets and **interactive** *whiteboards. A lesson might include playing a game on a computer. Some people think screens are good for the classroom. They say screens are a way to get students interested in a lesson. Other people think screens in the classroom are a problem. They argue screens are a distraction. Some studies have shown that technology in the classroom does not increase test scores. What are some positive and negative reasons for having screens in the classroom?*

CHAPTER 2

The Effects of Screen Addiction

Many professionals do not officially recognize screen addiction. Screen addiction is not like other mental illnesses. There is no official **diagnosis**. This can make it difficult for professionals to help people. It is not clear where the line is between healthy and unhealthy use. Too much screen time can have negative effects on someone's body, brain, and life. The impact of screen use mostly depends on how much time a person spends on screens and the **content** of what they are viewing.

Too much screen time can damage the body in many different ways. Being hunched over a computer or phone for long periods of time can lead to headaches, neck pain, and back pain. Eye problems can develop. Sitting for long periods is

At night, the light of a screen can trick the brain into thinking it is still day, leading to insomnia or poor sleep.

linked to many illnesses. This includes heart disease, diabetes, and cancer. When someone is spending most of their time on screens, they are not doing other activities that help them stay healthy and fit. Less sleep is another common outcome. Personal hygiene can also suffer. Weight gain and even obesity can be another symptom of screen addiction.

Around 25 percent of the time people spend online is on social media.

The effects of screens on mental health are linked to content. Social media is known to be particularly harmful. Social media use is linked to anxiety and depression. When people compare their lives to those they see on-screen, they can become deeply unhappy. Screen time has been shown to lower people's **attention span**. Ten years ago, the average attention span was 12 seconds. Today, it is 8 seconds. A goldfish has an attention span of 9 seconds.

When a post is liked or a video game level is beaten, people get a rush of good feeling. The feeling comes from their brain. The brain releases a **hormone** called dopamine. Over time, the brain becomes **dependent** on the dopamine. Then people crave screen time. This works the same way with other addictions, such as tobacco or alcohol.

Dangers of Distracted Driving

One of the most dangerous things a person can do is look at a screen while driving. It is like driving with your eyes closed. Every year, thousands of people are injured or killed from distracted driving. There have been many efforts to stop distracted driving. Most states have strict laws about using technology while driving. People are asked to pledge to not use their phones. Commercials share horror stories. Still, more than 25 percent of car crashes in the United States are due to cell phones. Can you think of other ways to solve this problem? Brainstorm a list of other methods. Be sure to include creative solutions.

The Warning Signs

It can be hard to tell if someone has a screen problem. It seems everyone is using devices all the time. There are many warning signs of screen addiction. People lose control of their screen use. They spend more time online than they planned. Sleep is lost and their health suffers. People at risk for screen addiction start to choose screen time over other things they like to do. They use screens even if it causes problems with friends, family, work, or school. It is important to be honest and aware of yourself and other people in your life. If you think you or a loved one might have a problem, reach out for help.

Screen addiction can harm people's social lives too. More time spent on screens means less time spent with friends and loved ones. Someone with screen addiction ignores other people in real life. Their personal relationships can suffer.

Sources of Screen Addiction

Video Games

Personal Computers

Tablets

Cell Phones

TV

Laptops

CHAPTER 3

Teens and Screen Addiction

Screens provide an easy way for teens to learn new information, keep up with friends, watch videos, and listen to music. This can lead to a lot of screen time. The average teen is on their phone 9 hours a day. About 54 percent of teens think they spend too much time with screens.

Teenagers use the internet to look up information and learn new things. This can help them with their studies. But teenagers that spend a lot of time with technology struggle at school. They have problems with attention and focus. They have low reading scores. These teens have higher rates of **ADHD** and angry, violent behavior. They also have higher rates of depression and anxiety. Without their phones, most teens report having negative feelings. They feel anxious, lonely, and upset. Screen

Tools such as fidget spinners and squeeze-balls can help with anxiety and attention, and keep the hands busy without technological devices.

use is also linked to a new condition. Professionals are calling it digital **malaise**. Teens are becoming less creative and less curious. Many don't care about engaging with the real world. Teens can develop digital malaise even with small amounts of screen time.

Social media is a popular way to communicate with friends. Yet screen use actually keeps teens from building communication skills. When you only write your feelings, you lose the ability to speak them. When you only read other people's words, you lose the ability to pick up on non-verbal cues.

Cyberbullying

Most teens encounter **cyberbullying**. *A cyberbully might send mean messages. Or a cyberbully might post an embarrassing photo of other people. Being a victim of cyberbullying can be very difficult emotionally and mentally. Some teens commit cyberbullying on accident. They forget to get other people's permission to post a photo. A teen might feel like someone is being mean to them online. So they are mean back. Sometimes humor does not come across well in messages. When posting something online, it is important to ask yourself questions. Does this single someone out? Could someone interpret it in a different way than I mean? How would I feel if I read this? Did I get permission to post this?*

Non-verbal cues include eye contact and facial expressions. Someone's gestures and body language also give important information. Not being able to read these cues can cause problems in relationships. This can lead to isolation, in the present and in the future.

When teens spend more time in front of a screen, they spend less time on healthy activities. They sleep less. They eat more junk food. Their overall health and fitness become worse. Screen addiction as a teen is also linked to other addictions as an adult. This includes tobacco and alcohol.

Screen time also exposes teens to hurtful and dangerous activity online. Almost 60 percent of teens are victims of cyberbullying. They are called names. False rumors are spread about them. While online, teens are bothered and threatened by other people. Sometimes they are bothered by strangers. Many teens run into inappropriate or even illegal content while online. The more time a teen spends online, the more they put themselves at risk.

How Much Is Too Much?

It can be hard for parents to decide how much time their kids should spend on screens. Many parents look to the American Academy of Pediatrics for advice. The group used to say 2 hours a day for kids ages 2 and older. In 2016, the guidelines were changed to 1 hour of screen time a day for kids 2–5. The time limits for older kids were removed. Some people think these suggestions are already outdated. They say 1 hour a day is not enough for young kids. Other people think the recommendations should be tighter. They want time limits for older kids. Why do you think the suggestions have changed? How can you choose how much screen time is right for you?

Solving Screen Addiction

Breaking an addiction to screens can be very difficult. A person with a screen addiction has to live surrounded by screens. Today, technology is essential to daily life. A screen addict must relearn to use technology in a healthy way. One of the hardest things they have to learn is how to live without being constantly **stimulated**.

The first step to recovery is to get help. This starts with talking to someone. It can be a parent or other family member. Or it can be a guidance counselor or teacher. The conversation needs to feel safe and comfortable. Sometimes people do not feel comfortable talking to someone they know. They can find information in books or online first.

When seeking help with an addiction, teens can reach out to a trusted adult or someone who has recovered from an addiction too.

People with screen addiction usually meet with a mental health counselor. Counselors work with patients to explore their screen use. Counselors try to identify what caused bad habits. Then they give patients tools for creating a better relationship with technology.

Science has shown that support groups are an effective way to maintain long-term recovery from addiction and trauma.

Many counselors suggest a "digital detox." This is when a person does not use any screen for 4 to 6 weeks. Some experts suggest a slow decrease of screen use. Others suggest people quit all at once. Then a person recovering from screen addiction can slowly start using screens again. They limit their use and practice healthy habits. They fill their time with social and physical activities.

After treatment, someone with screen addiction may still struggle. They might think about the internet and have urges to check their phones. Being around other people who are using screens can be difficult. Many people find being part of a group helps. Many addiction treatment centers have support groups. In these groups, people share their stories. They share ways to help maintain recovery.

Who Is to Blame?

Screen addiction is a new problem. Now people are debating over whose fault it is. Many people blame tech companies. They say tech companies' products are designed to be addictive. Other people say it's parents' responsibilities. Parents should be managing their children's screen use better. Or teachers need to be involved. Other people blame the screen addicts. These people think screen addicts should be able to manage their time and behavior better. People also argue about who is responsible for solving screen addiction. What do you think?

Keeping a journal can help people manage their behaviors, as well as work through emotions and problems.

Keeping Yourself Accountable

Most people are surprised to see how much time they spend on screens. A little here and there throughout the day really adds up. It is a good idea to check on your screen use. You can log your screen time by keeping a journal. Include the time of day, screen type, purpose, and length of time you spend on each screen. Then ask yourself questions. What was the purpose of this screen time? What did I gain? What did I lose? Was it a valuable use of my time? How could I accomplish this task with something that does not have a screen?

In many parts of the world, people do not have access to screens.
This leaves them with plenty of free time for fun activities.

CHAPTER 5

Making Healthy Choices

Everyone makes decisions about their screen use. For some people, this can become very difficult. They become dangerously addicted to technology. Most people find ways to use screens in a healthy way. Healthy screen users reduce time spent on screens for entertainment. They make wise choices and stay active physically.

There are many ways to lower your risk for screen addiction. You have to monitor and manage your screen use. Don't keep devices in your bedroom. This reduces staying up late or looking at them first thing in the morning. Don't use screens while eating. Create a screen-free time every day. Some people like to be screen-free after 5 p.m. For everything you do with a screen, there is an alternative. Instead of watching a show or

Instead of playing online games or video games, try playing board games with friends and loved ones.

movie, read a book. Instead of playing a video game, play a board game or cards. Try a new craft or hobby. Instead of using social media, spend time with your friends and family. Wear a watch to check the time. You can use a dictionary or encyclopedia to look up information. Or you can ask someone else your question. Creating a relaxing environment for yourself is important. This means turning off the TV and smartphone. Learn to be quiet and calm without distraction, and without the negative influence of the media.

Digital Detox

Anyone can do a digital detox. A digital detox can last one day, multiple days, or even a week. Be sure to have a conversation with your parents or guardians first. See if you can get your entire family on board. Then, put away any technology with a screen. You can cover a television with a sheet. Brainstorm other activities you can do and create a schedule to keep busy. Each day, keep a log of what you did to fill your time. Also report how you felt. Did you miss screens? How did you handle any negative feelings? Are you going to change your screen use habits?

Teens need to explore, define, and express themselves. The internet can be an amazing resource for teens. Screen use can help build lifelong skills. Writing a blog can improve your critical thinking and writing skills. Following the news and watching documentaries are great ways to raise your political and social awareness. You can learn new skills by following how-to videos and instructional websites. Screens can also be used for creative self-expression. Try using a computer to create your own media, such as videos, music, or artwork.

Screens have enabled many people to explore their creative sides in new and exciting ways.

When making choices, it is important to think about the effects screen time can have on your body and mind. It is important to know about the dangers and consequences of screen addiction. It is also important to think about your future. What are your priorities? What are your goals? How might they be affected by an addiction to screens? How can you balance the positive and negative effects of screens in your own life?

In-Person Communication

In-person communication can be difficult. Emails or texts may feel like an easy way out. But the conversations that are hard to have in-person are often the most important. You can improve your skills with practice. When having a conversation, make sure you are paying close attention. Do not look at a screen. It's okay to ask the person you are talking with to put away screens too. Pay attention to your body language. Do not cross your arms. Maintain eye contact. Think before you speak. Take just one moment to think about what you want to say. This is especially important if it is in response to the other person.

Research has shown that face-to-face communication leads to better outcomes.

Think About It

There are still many places in the world where people live without screens. In countries such as Guatemala, Uganda, Nepal, Turkmenistan, and Myanmar, less than 20 percent of people have access to the internet. Some people think that internet access is a human right. Other people think a traditional way of life is good too.

Choose a country from the list above. Research the country at your local library or online. What is life like for the average person? How do they keep busy? How do they get work done without screens? Do you think their lives could be improved with screen technology?

[21ST CENTURY SKILLS LIBRARY]

Learn More

BOOKS

Manocha, Ramesh. *Nurturing Young Minds: Mental Wellbeing in the Digital Age.* Generation Next. Sydney: Hachette Australia, 2018.

Orr, Tamra. *Social Networking.* Global Citizens: Social Media. North Mankato, MN: Cherry Lake Publishing, 2019.

Price, Catherine. *How to Break Up with Your Phone.* Berkeley: Ten Speed Press, 2018.

Skeen, Michelle. *Communication Skills for Teens: How to Listen, Express, and Connect for Success.* Oakland: Instant Help Books, 2016.

Steffens, Bradley. *Thinking Critically: Cell Phones.* San Diego: ReferencePoint Press, Inc., 2018.

ON THE WEB

TeensHealth
https://kidshealth.org/en/teens/internet-safety.html

Pew Research Center
http://www.pewinternet.org/2018/05/31/teens-social-media-technology-2018

Screen-Free Week
http://www.screenfree.org

The Center for Internet and Technology Addiction
https://virtual-addiction.com

GLOSSARY

addiction (uh-DIK-shun) having no control over doing something, such as drugs or gambling, even though you know it is bad for your health and life

ADHD (AYE-dee-h-dee) a mental health issue that makes a person have trouble paying attention or sitting still; stands for attention deficit hyperactivity disorder

attention span (uh-TEN-shuhn SPAEHN) how long a person can focus on any one thing

content (KAHN-tent) the topics, ideas, and images that are included in a piece of work

cyberbullying (SY-buhr-bul-lee-ing) act of posting insulting, embarassing, or hurtful messages or photos of another person on the internet

dependent (dee-PEN-duhnt) needing an outside source or substance to keep working

diagnosis (dy-ig-NOH-suhs) a doctor's conclusion about what is causing a patient's symptoms

hormone (HOR-mohn) a chemical made by the body that influences the brain and bodily functions

interactive (in-tur-AK-tiv) allowing a person to control and change what is happening on a computer or other piece of technology

malaise (muh-LAYZ) a feeling of tiredness, unhappiness, and lack of energy

social media (SOH-shul MEE-dee-uh) websites and applications through which people can communicate and share ideas using the internet

stimulated (STIM-yoo-lay-tid) inspired, excited, or entertained by something

INDEX